Preparing for Group Assignments at University and College

The Workbook

Adam Morgan

Sydney, Australia

Published 2024 by Adam Morgan

All rights reserved. Except to the extent permitted by law, no part of this publication may be reproduced, distributed, or transmitted in any form or by any means, including photocopying, recording, or other electronic or mechanical methods, without the prior written permission of the author. For permission requests, contact via preparing-for-group-assignments.com.

The information contained in this workbook is for educational purposes. No warranties of any kind are declared or implied. By engaging with this workbook, the user agrees that under no circumstances is the author responsible for any damages or losses, direct or indirect, that are incurred as a result of the use of the information contained within this workbook, including, but not limited to, errors, omissions, or inaccuracies.

ISBN 978-0-6456794-3-4

Copyright © 2024 Adam Morgan

Design and Layout:
Ilka Staudinger-Morgan

Contents

Introduction ... 1

Part A: Considering Your Upcoming Experiences ... 3

    1. Group Growth Over Time – Tuckman ... 4

    2. Group Growth Over Time – Weber ... 5

    3. Setting Norms ... 6

    4. Making Collective Decisions ... 7

    5. Behaving and Responding Cycles ... 8

    6. Reduction in Behaviors ... 9

    7. Varying Outputs ... 10

    8. Conflict ... 11

    9. Positive Aspects ... 12

Part B: Considering the Bigger Picture ... 13

    10. Growth ... 14

    11. Documenting Group Experiences and Growth ... 15

    12. Starting Positively ... 16

    13. Taking Responsibility for Your Actions ... 17

    14. Diversity ... 18

    15. Support ... 19

Conclusion ... 21

References ... 22

Introduction

If you are reading these words, you have probably just finished reading *Preparing for Group Assignments at University and College: A Guide for Commencing Students*. If you have not done this, it is important that you first read the above-mentioned guide. This workbook builds on the topics and issues presented in the guide and assumes that you have engaged with its contents.

As you read the guide, you were probably thinking about your own upcoming group assignments. Hopefully, you were also thinking about the challenges and opportunities associated with group assignments presented in the guide. It is now time to think about your upcoming group experiences deeper. Reading about the challenges and opportunities associated with group assignments is one thing. Giving targeted thought to them is the next level.

As an overview, this workbook is divided into two main parts and mirrors the guide's structure. In the first part, we will re-visit the upcoming experiences presented in the guide. In the second part, we will cover some of the issues and suggestions offered in the guide's bigger picture section. In both parts, you will need to answer some prompting questions related to various topics and issues.

In terms of the quantity and quality of your entries, this is largely your decision. However, if the completion of this workbook is a requirement at your institution, there might be specific expectations regarding the quantity and quality of your entries. If the completion of this workbook is a requirement, it is important that you clarify what these expectations are before making your entries.

Part A

Considering Your Upcoming Experiences

In the guide, we covered some of the main things that you will probably experience when doing group assignments. These were:

- Group growth over time
- Setting norms
- Making collective decisions
- Behaving and responding cycles
- Reduction in behaviors
- Varying outputs
- Conflict
- Positive aspects

As each was presented, you were hopefully thinking about your upcoming group assignments and the extent to which various issues might eventuate. It is now time to give each a little more consideration.

1. Group Growth Over Time – Tuckman

In the guide, group growth over time was the first topic covered. One model presented was Tuckman's (1965; Tuckman & Jensen, 1977), which has the following stages: forming, storming, norming, performing, and adjourning.

What will be the main challenges getting your assignment groups to the performing stage?

How will you help your assignment groups make it to the performing stage in a good way?

2. Group Growth Over Time – Weber

The other growth model presented in the guide was Weber's (1982) life cycle model, which comprises the following stages: birth, infancy, adolescence, adulthood, and death. Just like humans, it was suggested that groups are born, develop into adulthood, and will eventually die.

What will be the challenges when your assignment groups reach the adolescence stage?

How will you help nurture your newly-born assignment groups?

3. Setting Norms

Setting norms was the next topic covered in the guide. It was suggested that social behaviors are often governed by norms. Sometimes norms are expressed in relation to what people 'should do' (e.g., standing in line, waiting to be served). On other occasions, norms are expressed in relation to what people 'should not do' (e.g., cutting into the line). The way people behave in groups is also governed by norms. These norms are set by the group and help the group to function.

What are some of the main norms you would like to see established in your assignment groups?

How will you help your assignment groups establish strong norms?

4. Making Collective Decisions

Making collective decisions was the next topic covered in the guide. It was suggested that groups need to make many collective decisions. However, making these decisions can be challenging due to various problems that can occur. Three decision-making problems were presented in the guide: 1) making a decision that no member wants, 2) making a decision that ignores concerns, and 3) making a decision that satisfies the wishes of the powerful minority.

Which of the above-mentioned problems are you most worried about experiencing in your assignment groups and why?

How will you help your assignment groups make good collective decisions?

5. Behaving and Responding Cycles

Next, behaving and responding cycles were covered in the guide. It was suggested that much of what is seen in groups are cycles comprised of behaving and responding. Sometimes these cycles are positive. A member will behave in a positive way (e.g., helping). The responses from others will also be positive. Sometimes, however, the opposite will occur. The behaviors of members will be seen less positively and will elicit different types of responses (e.g., disapproval, annoyance).

What types of positive behaving and responding cycles are you hoping to see a lot of in your assignment groups?

How will you go about maximizing the emergence of positive behaving and responding cycles in your assignment groups?

6. Reduction in Behaviors

Reduction in behaviors was the next topic covered in the guide. It was suggested that the reduction in behaviors is quite common in assignment groups. Sometimes this reduction is linked to a member's inability to fully participate. On other occasions, the reduction appears more strategic. A member has the potential to fully participate but does not do so for various reasons.

What concerns you the most about the reduction in members' behaviors in your assignment groups?

How will you go about addressing the reduction in members' behaviors in your assignment groups?

7. Varying Outputs

Varying outputs was the next topic covered in the guide. The generation of outputs is an important part of group assignments. Typically, all members are meant to generate these outputs. It was suggested that the quality of these outputs can often vary. Sometimes a member will produce high quality work. Sometimes, however, the work produced by a member might be perceived as being very poor.

What concerns you the most about members producing poor quality work in your assignment groups?

What will you do if members produce poor quality work in your assignment groups?

8. Conflict

Conflict was the next topic covered in the guide. It was suggested that groups often experience conflict. It was also suggested that three different types of conflict exist in groups: 1) task conflict, 2) process conflict, and 3) relationship conflict.

Which of the above-mentioned conflict types are you most worried about experiencing in your assignment groups and why?

How will you go about navigating conflict in your assignment groups?

9. Positive Aspects

Finally, the guide covered some of the many positive aspects that you might experience in your assignment groups. However, it was suggested that these positive aspects are not guaranteed to arise. Rather, they need to be fostered. The positive aspects covered in the guide were 1) synergy, 2) helping/backing up behavior, 3) group cohesion, 4) collective efficacy/group potency, 5) group viability, and 6) safety.

Which of the above-mentioned positive aspects would you like to experience a lot of in your assignment groups and why?

How will you go about fostering the emergence of positive aspects in your assignment groups?

Part B

Considering the Bigger Picture

In the guide's bigger picture part, some important suggestions were offered to you. These were:

- View group work as a growth opportunity
- Know where you need to grow
- Document your group experiences and growth
- Start positively
- Take responsibility for your actions
- Embrace diversity
- Seek support

It is now time to give each of these suggestions some deeper consideration.

10. Growth

It was suggested that your group work experiences will provide you with the opportunity to grow. This is particularly the case with the development of your teamworking abilities (see the guide for specific abilities). It was also suggested that you should consider two areas related to your growth: 1) the aspects of group work you are already quite good at, and 2) those aspects in need of further improvement.

Which aspects of group work are you already quite good at?

Which aspects of group work do you still need to improve?

11. Documenting Group Experiences and Growth

Next, it was suggested that you should consider documenting your group experiences and growth. It was suggested that sometime in the future you might need to describe your teamworking abilities, group experiences, and growth. It was also suggested that relying on memory to do this is challenging. Documenting your group experiences and growth, and keeping these documents in a folder was recommended.

What will be the challenges of documenting your group experiences and growth?

How will you go about starting your group experiences and growth folder?

12. Starting Positively

Next, it was suggested that starting positively is important in group work. It was suggested that each of your assignment groups will have the potential to start positively. It just requires each member to make a conscious effort to act pro-socially in the initial interactions.

What will be the benefits of members starting positively in your assignment groups?

How will you contribute to positive starts in your assignment groups?

13. Taking Responsibility for Your Actions

Next, it was suggested that group members need to take responsibility for their actions. It was suggested that members of assignment groups are interdependent. Each member's actions impact the other members of the group. Each member needs to recognize this and take responsibility for their actions.

What would your assignment groups look like if all members were to take responsibility for their actions?

Why should you take responsibility for your actions in your assignment groups?

14. Diversity

Next, it was suggested that groups in higher education settings are comprised of diverse members. You will be working in diverse groups. This is not new to you, as you have been in diverse groups before. But groups at university and college can be particularly diverse.

What will be the challenges of working in diverse groups at your institution?

What will be the benefits of working in diverse groups at your institution?

15. Support

The final suggestion offered in the guide concerned the seeking of support. It was suggested that your institution has a duty of care for your well-being and is there to support you with your group assignments. However, it was also suggested that you will need to seek support, as teachers and staff at your institution will probably be unaware that you are having issues in a group.

In what ways would you like to see your institution support you with your group assignments?*

*see over

When will you seek support?

*It is important that the staff at your institution know how you would like to be supported. What you have written here reflects this. Let your teachers and support staff know. Let your institution's senior leaders know. They are always interested in hearing your ideas around support.

Conclusion

Group assignments will be a part of your upcoming student experience. The purpose of this workbook is to help you further prepare for this type of group work. *Preparing for Group Assignments at University and College: A Guide for Commencing Students* provided an overview of the relevant topics and issues surrounding this type of group work. Reading the guide was the first step in the preparation process. This workbook has been the next step. It has given you the opportunity to think deeper about your upcoming group assignments. Hopefully, you have given deeper consideration to the topics and issues you will face and feel even more prepared for your upcoming group assignment journeys.

For your next steps, you should review what you have written in this workbook. You should also consider how you will implement what you have written. This will help you further prepare for your upcoming group assignments. Finally, you should put your completed workbook in a safe place (e.g., in your group experiences and growth folder). It is a record of your thoughts at a particular point in time. They have been captured in this workbook and might be needed in the future. For example, you might need to bring your completed workbook to a class or session for discussion. You might also need to look back at your entries in the future (e.g., as part of a final-year reflective task). As you put your completed workbook in that safe place, take a moment to recognize what you have done. You have engaged with an important part of your upcoming student experience–group assignments. By doing so, you have shown a commitment to enhancing both your student experience and those of your peers. It is now time to demonstrate this commitment and see the benefits.

References

Tuckman, B. W. (1965). Developmental sequences in small groups. *Psychological Bulletin, 63,* 384-399.

Tuckman, B. W., & Jensen, M. A. C. (1977). Stages of small group development revisited. *Group and Organizational Management, 2,* 419-427.

Weber, R. C. (1982). The group: A cycle from birth to death. In L. Porter & B. Mohr (Eds.), *NTL readings guide for human relations training.* Arlington, VA: NTL Institute.

Name:

Date of completion:

Other information if needed (e.g., institution, class, student number):

Preparing for Group Assignments: The Workbook | 23

www.ingramcontent.com/pod-product-compliance
Lightning Source LLC
Chambersburg PA
CBHW051159290426
44109CB00022B/2513